What Were the Twin Towers?

by Jim O'Connor

illustrated by Ted Hammond

SCHOLASTIC INC.

For all the brave first responders on 9/11—JOC

For my mom—TH

ISBN 978-1-338-10028-0

Contents

What Were the Twin Towers?

It was a perfect end-of-summer morning in New York City. The sky was a clear, rich blue and there were no clouds.

At the tip of Manhattan, by 8:20 a.m., people were streaming in from subways and from Staten Island ferryboats. The World Trade Center's Twin Towers gleamed in the sunlight. The North Tower and the South Tower. Some office workers lingered in the tree-lined plaza at the base of the buildings.

Many people were already upstairs at their desks starting work. At the famous Windows on the World restaurant, several companies were hosting business breakfasts. The restaurant was in the North Tower, on the 106th and 107th floors. The view was spectacular that morning. Diners could see more than fifty miles in any direction.

It was just another normal morning. Then at 8:46, everything changed. People on the street heard a roar. They looked up to see a jet airplane overhead. It was flying low, dangerously low. And it was heading straight toward the North Tower. In a matter of seconds, it slammed into floors ninety-three through ninety-nine.

This was the first blow of a terrible attack on the United States of America. In the next seventy-seven minutes, a second plane hit the South Tower. A third plane flew into the Pentagon building just outside of Washington, DC. A fourth plane crashed in central Pennsylvania. Everyone in all

four planes was killed, including the nineteen men who had hijacked the flights and carried out the attacks.

By 10:28 that morning, both towers had collapsed, killing 2,606 innocent people. Another 125 died at the Pentagon. In all, 2,977 died on September 11, 2001, counting the passengers and crew on all four planes.

In the months and years that followed, there would be more victims. Many were rescue workers—police officers and firefighters—as well as construction workers who came to clean up the site. They became sick from breathing the polluted air while working at Ground Zero. That became the name for the area where the Twin Towers had once stood.

Why were the Twin Towers targeted? Who was behind the attack? And how did that terrible day change the United States?

CHAPTER 1
Money, Money, Money

More than any other city in the United States, New York has always been a center of business. In America in the 1600s and 1700s, many colonies were founded by groups seeking religious freedom. But not New York. It began as a Dutch trading post called New Amsterdam. Its purpose was to make money.

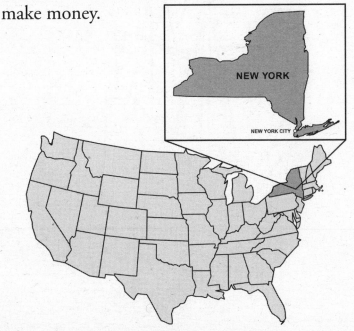

NEW YORK

NEW YORK CITY

The Dutch took advantage of the large natural harbor that stayed ice-free all winter. This meant that ships with cargo could come and go all year. And the Hudson River, to the west of New Amsterdam, offered a route to fur trading posts farther inland.

The British forced the Dutch out of New Amsterdam in 1664 and renamed it New York. They stayed over a hundred years, until the end of the Revolutionary War in 1783. After that, New York City became the trading center of a new, young country: the United States of America.

Manhattan, where New York City began, is an island. Because of that, over time six bridges as well as four tunnels—two under the East River and two under the Hudson—were constructed to connect Manhattan to mainland areas.

Many of these transportation routes are overseen
by an agency called the Port Authority of New
York & New Jersey. It has control over the port,
covering a twenty-five-mile circle, with the Statue
of Liberty at the center. Tolls from bridges and

tunnels provide the money for more new projects. In the middle of the twentieth century, the Port Authority headed the biggest building project in New York's history—the construction of two skyscrapers, each 110 stories. They were the tallest buildings on the planet—at least for a while.

CHAPTER 2
Sky-high Towers

The idea for the World Trade Center was hatched in the brain of a very rich banker. His name was David Rockefeller. He was the president of Chase Manhattan Bank, one of the largest banks in the world.

David Rockefeller

In 1960, Rockefeller built a new headquarters for the bank. It was a sixty-story, glass-and-steel skyscraper in Lower Manhattan near Wall Street. This area was often called the dullest part of Manhattan. It was full of older office

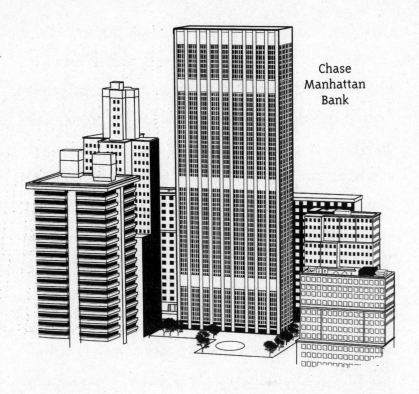

Chase
Manhattan
Bank

buildings for law firms and accounting companies.
At night, it was a ghost town.

David Rockefeller wanted Lower Manhattan
to attract all kinds of businesses and become a
lively neighborhood. He couldn't afford to build
more big skyscrapers by himself, so he approached
the Port Authority to help with the project.

It was smart of Rockefeller to ask the Port Authority. It had a special power called *eminent domain*. This meant it could get rid of privately owned buildings to make way for its projects. It didn't matter if there were homes or businesses where it wanted to build. They would be torn down.

When the new project—called the World Trade Center—was proposed, the Port Authority used eminent domain to get the land it needed.

By the fall of 1961, a plan called for the World Trade Center to be built over a railway terminal that linked Manhattan to New Jersey. The location was a twelve-block square near the Hudson River. That's as big as seventy-four football fields!

Most of the site was covered by old low buildings, some brick houses, garages, and lofts. They would all have to be knocked down. Would anybody really mind if those buildings were torn down to make way for the Trade Center?

Yes! There turned out to be a lot of opposition to the plan.

Part of the area was known as "Radio Row" because so many stores sold or repaired radios and electronics. Small business owners tried to stop the project. Owners of office buildings were also against the plan. With so much new office space available—ten million square feet—rents would drop in the older buildings in the area. Landlords would lose money.

But there was also strong support for the project. Following a 1962 speech, President John F. Kennedy said that the Trade Center would be good for the country's economy. Yet even with backing from a president, big projects do not happen one, two, three. The World Trade Center did get approved. But the process dragged on more than five years, from March 1961 to August 1966.

John F. Kennedy

New York City was going to get two new giant buildings. Still, city officials wanted something more for so much disruption in the area.

The head of the Port Authority was a man named Austin J. Tobin. He came up with an idea. All the dirt dug up in the process of building the World Trade Center would be trucked a few blocks away. Then it would be dumped into the Hudson River. This would create twenty-three acres of new land for Manhattan. New York City would own the land and could either sell or develop it.

Tobin's idea was very clever. New York City got free new land and the Port Authority didn't have to pay for all that dirt to be carted to some faraway place.

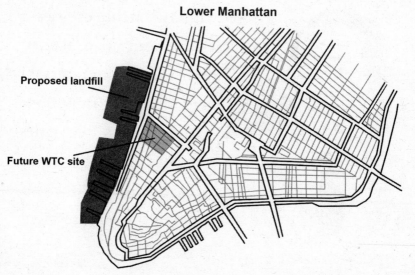

Lower Manhattan

Proposed landfill

Future WTC site

Finally, the project was approved and ready to go. Except for one thing. There was no definite plan for the buildings. In fact, an architect had not even been chosen.

The Port Authority asked seven firms of architects to offer ideas. The organization told the architects that their plans had to create a "city within a city," with at least ten million square feet of space to rent and towers at least one hundred stories tall. It had to have an outdoor plaza for visitors and workers, an underground shopping mall, and a link to local subways and railways.

Minoru Yamasaki

The winning architect was a Japanese-American man named Minoru Yamasaki. Yamasaki had designed important buildings in big cities before, but the Trade Center would be his largest by far. He spent months drawing and making models. His final plan showed two towers with a large plaza. Several "smaller" big buildings were spread around the site. The towers that he'd planned, however, were no taller than eighty floors. And they would have only eight million square feet of rental space.

The man in charge of the project was named Guy F. Tozzoli. "Yama," Tozzoli said, "President Kennedy is going to put a man on the moon. You're going to figure out a way to build me the tallest buildings in the world."

Guy F. Tozzoli

Yamasaki went back to his drawing board. His new design had towers that were each 110 stories. Now the Trade Center would have the ten million square feet of office space.

Guy F. Tozzoli gave the okay.

CHAPTER 3
Battle Plan

Now someone had to take Yamasaki's plans and turn them into real buildings. Guy F. Tozzoli chose an engineer named Ray Monti to be the construction manager.

Monti was a great choice. He had been in the navy and ran the project like a military battle. He had a detailed plan of action that followed a just-in-time schedule. That meant all the pieces

of the buildings—I-beams, pipes, wiring, even the bolts to hold everything together—would arrive at exactly the moment they were needed.

The first part of the project started March 21, 1966, when crews began tearing down all the old buildings on the site. After that, the crew dug down seventy feet until they reached bedrock. *Bedrock* is the layer of superhard rock beneath the soil. That was where the bases of the towers would rest.

The Hudson River was only seven hundred feet away. Half of the site was where the river had once run, way back when New York was called New Amsterdam. Over the next three hundred years, the Hudson had been pushed west by landfill—old piers, dirt, junk, and even some old buildings. The engineers needed to be sure river water would not seep into the construction site. So they built what came to be called a *slurry wall* just west of the towers.

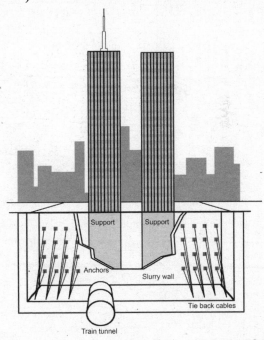

They dug trenches twenty-two feet long, three feet wide, and sixty-five feet deep. As they dug, they pumped a mixture of water and gray clay called *slurry* into the trenches. Then they lowered a twenty-five-ton steel cage into each trench and filled it with concrete. They forced the slurry

mixture up and out, where it could be used for the next piece of the wall. Over the next fourteen months, crews repeated the process more than 150 times to surround an area that was four blocks long and two blocks wide. It was called the *bathtub*. It would prevent any Hudson River water from coming into the construction site. Now the actual building could begin.

CHAPTER 4
Up They Go

Crews first laid a concrete base for forty-seven columns that would support the elevators in each tower. The elevator area formed the center, or core, for each building. The *core* also had space for utility areas, restrooms, and three staircases. Another 236 columns would support the outside walls of each building.

Once all of the columns were put in place, constructing the steel structure of the buildings began. By the spring of 1969, steel was in place for the North Tower core up to the ninth floor.

Yamasaki designed the two towers without columns breaking up floor space inside. This was very different from older skyscrapers. Every floor in the towers was an acre in size. A huge, open area went from the elevators to the outside walls. Tenants could design office spaces any way they wanted.

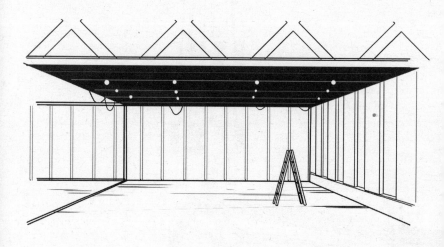

The outside walls were load-bearing. This meant the walls helped hold up the building. Each wall unit was made of steel panels that weighed twenty-two tons!

The elevator core and outside walls were built at the same time. After the walls went up, the floors were put in. Then electricians, carpenters, and plumbers began their work.

The Port Authority knew that erecting two 110-story buildings was an incredible challenge.

Kangaroo crane

For the World Trade Center towers, a new kind of crane was used. It came from Australia and was nicknamed the "kangaroo crane." It made the job easier and faster.

Before this, smaller skyscrapers were built with either derricks or crawling cranes. The crawling cranes had worked in front of the construction site, lifting up materials to workers. The cranes, however, were dangerous. Sometimes they collapsed.

Also, they could lift loads only as high as the length of the crane's arm. Derricks were built onto a landing of a building and lifted material up only as far as the next floor. Once that floor was finished, the derrick

had to be taken apart and moved up. The whole process took a day and a half and was very tricky.

Kangaroo cranes had a 120-foot tower that ended in an operator's cabin with an arm stretching out over the edge of the building. The "hopping" came from jacks under the cabin that lifted it up as far as twenty feet at a time. The crane could lift three floors' worth of steel.

Once new tower sections were bolted into place, the crane hopped another twenty feet. And one more time. The process was much quicker than taking a derrick apart and moving it. Once the building was finished, the kangaroo crane lifted a smaller crane to the roof. Then workmen took the kangaroo crane apart and the pieces were lowered to the street.

The final step in construction was attaching a stylish aluminum "skin" to the outside of the buildings. This skin is called a *curtain wall*. It keeps cold or warm air inside the building and bad weather outside.

As for windows, the Trade Center's were bronze-tinted glass only twenty-two inches wide. Each window was set ten inches deep into the building. This made for a more interesting look than just a plain, flat surface. Together, the Twin Towers had 43,600 windows.

Of course, the bigger a building is, the more people can work there. But more people mean more elevators. And elevators take up lots of space.

How could the Trade Center elevators handle the 150,000 workers and visitors expected to come and go each day?

A Port Authority architect came up with a smart plan. Each tower was divided into three zones. Zone One went up to the forty-fourth floor. Zone Two went up from the forty-fourth floor to the seventy-eighth floor. Zone Three went from the seventy-eighth floor to the 110th.

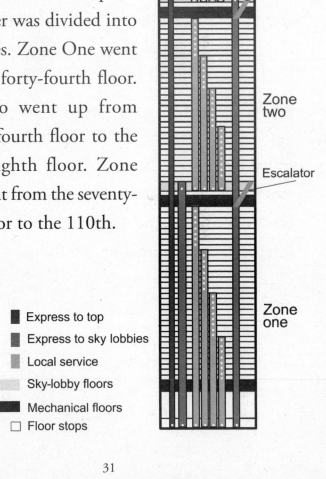

110 floors

Zone three

Escalator

Zone two

Escalator

Zone one

■ Express to top
■ Express to sky lobbies
▮ Local service
▯ Sky-lobby floors
■ Mechanical floors
□ Floor stops

Each zone had elevators that only served its floors. But there were also going to be express elevators. Some went from the lobby to either the forty-fourth floor or the seventy-eighth floor. And a couple went straight to the 110th floor. So if someone worked on the sixty-sixth floor, she would take an express elevator to the forty-fourth floor, then a local elevator to the sixy-sixth floor.

The zone plan allowed elevator cars serving different zones to use the same elevator shaft. This cut down on space. The final plan for each tower called for twenty-three express elevators, seventy-two locals, and nine freight elevators. The freight elevators also served basements, which had six levels. That was a total of 116 floors.

CHAPTER 5
Love 'em or Hate 'em!

The first tenants moved into the North Tower in December 1970. Tenants moved into the South Tower beginning in September 1971. This was before the official opening. The Port Authority was eager to collect rent as soon as possible.

The big opening day was April 4, 1973. Even then, the Twin Towers were not completely finished, but almost ten thousand people already worked inside them. The governors of New York and New Jersey both spoke at the ceremony in the lobby of the North Tower. Nelson Rockefeller,

New York's governor, was the brother of David Rockefeller, who had first dreamed of building giant skyscrapers in the neighborhood.

Criticism of the towers came at once. One critic called them "just glass-and-metal filing cabinets." Another said they looked like the "boxes the Empire State Building and Chrysler Building came in." Plus, they had cost so much—$800 million, far above the Port Authority's original estimate of $350 million.

The Port Authority announced that the complex was 80 percent rented—a big success. But real-estate developers pointed out that a lot of tenants were large government agencies. They had "sweetheart deals." This meant they were paying much lower rents than they would have elsewhere.

But no matter if people loved the Twin Towers or hated them, New York City now had two giant new landmarks.

New York City's Tallest Buildings

New York City has a long history of building skyscrapers that, at one time or another, were the tallest in the world.

Built in 1930, the Chrysler Building (1,046 feet tall) may be New York City's most beautiful building. However, it was its tallest for only eleven months.

Built in 1931, the Empire State Building (1,250 feet tall) beat out the Chrysler for the title of tallest. One of the most famous buildings in the world, it remains a symbol of New York City.

The Twin Towers (1,368 feet tall) displaced the Empire State Building as the tallest in the world until Chicago's Sears Tower opened in 1973.

Finished in 2013, One World Trade Center (1,776 feet tall) is often called the Freedom Tower and is currently the tallest building in New York City.

As of 2015, the tallest completed building in the world was Burj Khalifa in Dubai. It is 2,716.5 feet tall and has 163 floors.

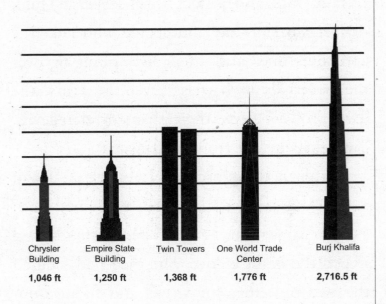

Chrysler Building	Empire State Building	Twin Towers	One World Trade Center	Burj Khalifa
1,046 ft	**1,250 ft**	**1,368 ft**	**1,776 ft**	**2,716.5 ft**

CHAPTER 6
Daredevils

All famous landmarks attract tourists. But certain ones also attract thrill-seekers. Think of Niagara Falls and the people who risked—and sometimes lost—their lives plunging over the waterfalls in barrels. Over the years, the Twin Towers drew their share of daredevils. Two incidents are truly amazing.

Early on the morning of August 7, 1974, a tightrope walker from France stepped onto a wire cable that he and some friends had rigged the night before. The men had scouted the two buildings for weeks and figured out how to get up to the roofs without being seen. They used a bow and arrow to send a small rope from one tower to the other.

Then they pulled bigger and heavier ropes across until they were able to string the tightrope.

This was no ordinary circus act. The wire ran between the World Trade Center's North and South Towers. The stuntman's name was Philippe Petit. For forty-five minutes, Petit stayed 1,350 feet above the ground. That's more than a quarter of a mile high! And there was no safety net. If he fell, it was all over.

Down below, a huge crowd gathered. Petit made eight trips. One time he stopped and lay down on the wire. Another time he danced on it. He also knelt and saluted people, including the New York City police, who were watching him.

Was there an accident? Happily, no.

It was the first—and also the last—time anyone attempted to get from the North Tower to the South Tower this way!

Petit's performance ended with his arrest. The charges, however, were dropped when he agreed to give a free performance for children in Central Park. In 2008, a documentary called *Man on Wire* told the story of Petit's amazing feat at the World Trade Center. Watching it, even though you know there was no accident, you feel as though your heart is in your throat!

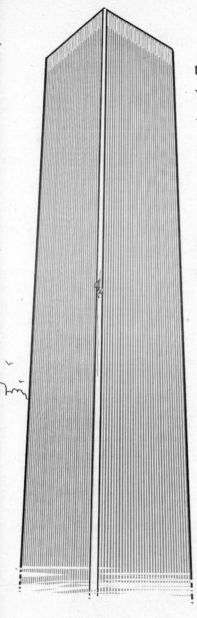

Instead of walking between the towers, a Queens, New York, man named George Willig decided to climb the outside of the South Tower. Willig was a mountain climber and had spent a year examining the tower and planning his stunt.

He began at six thirty on the morning of May 26, 1977. Willig had designed special clamps that fit into the tracks made for window-washing platforms. When he leaned back, the clamps tightened and held him in place. Then Willig could place the next clamp higher and continue up.

Two policemen on a window-washing platform managed to reach him. They tried to talk him out of the climb. One of the policemen was a suicide expert. After deciding that Willig knew what he was doing, the police let him continue.

Willig's climb took three and a half hours. When he was finished, he, too, was arrested, like Philippe Petit. The mayor of New York City fined Willig $1.10—a penny for every floor!

CHAPTER 7
City within a City

The World Trade Center was truly a "city within a city."

So much mail came to the Trade Center complex that it had its own zip code: 10048. On an average day, as many as 150,000 people visited the towers. Some came to do business with the many companies located there. Others visited merely to marvel at the sheer size of the buildings. In the South Tower, called Two World Trade Center, tourists paid to take a superfast express elevator to the 107th-floor indoor observatory. There was also an outdoor viewing deck on the roof. The view was awesome.

The North Tower, or One World Trade Center, had a much more expensive tourist attraction. The Windows on the World restaurant was on the 106th and 107th floors. It offered fancy food along with the views.

Each morning, about fifty thousand Trade Center workers poured out of city subways and New Jersey trains that stopped below the buildings. They grabbed coffee at fast-food restaurants in the underground shopping level to take to their desks. On nice days, they enjoyed their snacks or lunch outside in the Austin J. Tobin Plaza.

Besides the office workers, thousands of men and women kept the Trade Center humming day after day. There were window washers whose jobs never ended. Once every window was washed in

the two towers, the whole process had to start all over again. Cleaning crews kept the building shiny and bright. Engineers, electricians, and plumbers repaired equipment.

The Trade Center also had its own police force with all the powers of New York City police officers. The underground level had exactly what you'd expect to find at any shopping mall:

dress shops, shoe stores, card shops, bookstores, and many others. Because most customers were commuters, the stores opened earlier, around 8:00 a.m., before the workday began.

The Trade Center was much quieter at night. The neighborhood didn't become the lively 24-7 area that David Rockefeller had hoped for. Still, the towers were never empty. Besides the overnight cleaning crews, plumbers, electricians, and many security workers, there were people who worked at companies that tracked the stock markets in Hong Kong, Tokyo, and other cities many time zones and half a world away.

By 6:00 a.m., when some of the overnight workers were heading home, the first of the daytime workers were streaming out of the subways and trains again.

CHAPTER 8
The First Attack

If you ask anyone, *When were the Twin Towers attacked?* the answer is almost always September 11, 2001. But years earlier, on February 26, 1993, a small group of plotters tried to destroy the North Tower.

Ramzi Yousef was in a rented van packed with 1,200 pounds of explosives that stopped in the parking garage. Yousef and his driver left the van and hurried away.

A few minutes later, the van exploded. It blew a hole through five underground levels of the building and killed six people. The North Tower was badly damaged. The slurry wall at the base of the tower was cracked. The fire-alarm system broke.

Besides the damage and awful loss of life, this first attack revealed some serious problems in the Twin Towers. As with most other parking garages at the time, there had been no security officers. So anyone could get in and out. Nor did stairwells have emergency lighting. On the day of the explosion, thousands of employees had to walk down many flights of stairs in darkness.

Yousef was later captured in Pakistan. He was brought to trial in New York City. He admitted belonging to a group called Al Qaeda, which hated the United States. His plan was to cause so much damage to the North Tower that it would fall into the South Tower and destroy it, too. Why? To Yousef and Al Qaeda, the Trade Center represented the terrible worship of money and greed in the United States, a country they hoped to destroy.

In November 1997, Yousef was convicted of murder and conspiracy. He is in prison in Colorado, where he will remain for the rest of his life.

A memorial pool for the six victims of the bombing was built in the plaza in 1995. However, the attack on September 11, 2001, destroyed it. Now the names of the 1993 victims appear with the victims of September 11, both on the rim of one of the memorial fountains and inside the National September 11 Memorial & Museum.

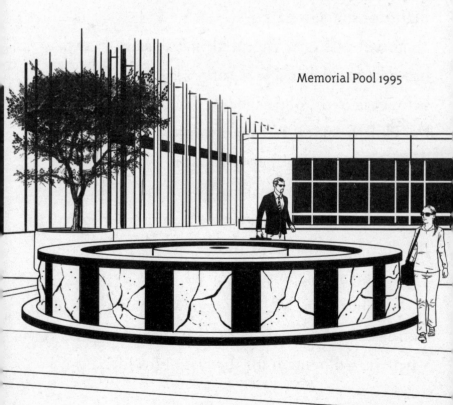

Memorial Pool 1995

What Is a Terrorist?

A terrorist may act alone, but usually belongs to a group that has declared itself the enemy of a country or government. Terrorists and terrorist groups will attack or use other forms of terror to weaken or destroy their enemies. Al Qaeda is a terrorist group. It was behind both the first attack on the North Tower in 1993 and the destruction of both towers in September 2001, as well as the plane crash into the Pentagon building and the plane wreck in Pennsylvania. It is believed that the last plane had been heading for either the White House or the Capitol in Washington, DC.

CHAPTER 9
9/11

September 11, 2001, was a day that changed not only the United States, but the entire world. The second Al Qaeda attack was different from the 1993 bombing of the North Tower. That was carried out by a small group of terrorists, with two men driving an explosive-filled van into the North Tower's parking garage. The 9/11 attacks involved nineteen men who split into four teams.

Together, they hijacked four jets and turned them into giant bombs. The attack was well planned and accomplished almost everything Al Qaeda set out to do.

Al Qaeda

Al Qaeda was founded in the late 1980s by Osama bin Laden and other terrorists. Born in 1957, bin Laden was the son of a wealthy Saudi Arabian businessman. In 1979, bin Laden joined a rebel group fighting in Afghanistan. He got others to join. And he also gave a great deal of money to buy weapons for the rebels.

Osama bin Laden

Al Qaeda members belong to the religion of Islam. Islam is a peaceful, loving religion with more than 1.6 billion followers worldwide. These followers are called *Muslims*, and about 3.4 million live in the United States.

Islam has never been in favor of terrorism. Yet Al Qaeda members believe that killing enemies is holy work. Members of Al Qaeda believe there is a Christian-Jewish alliance trying to destroy Islam. Osama bin Laden believed that the United States was the leader of the alliance. That was the reason for his hatred.

After the attacks on September 11, the United States searched for Osama bin Laden for almost ten years. Finally, he was killed by a team of US Navy SEALS in 2011, in a raid on the house where he was hiding in Pakistan.

Bin Laden approved a plan to hijack passenger jets and fly them into buildings that symbolized the United States. In New York City, the targets were the Twin Towers. In Washington, DC, the targets were the Pentagon, which is headquarters for the US military, and possibly either the White House or the Capitol Building, where the Senate and House of Representatives meet.

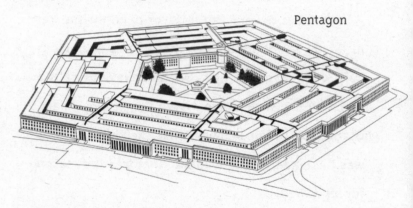
Pentagon

Osama bin Laden selected four men to move to the United States and learn to fly passenger planes. They would not bother learning how to land the planes, because they would be crashing them into buildings. Other men in Al Qaeda were trained to take over the crew and keep control of the passengers so that the hijackers could fly the planes to their targets.

Four flights were chosen. Each was leaving the East Coast for California. All the targeted buildings were on the East Coast, so the planes would not be in the air for long. They would be almost completely full of fuel when they crashed. More fuel meant a bigger explosion and more damage.

American Airlines Flight 11 flew out of Boston's Logan Airport at 7:59 a.m. About forty-seven minutes later, it reached its target. People near the Twin Towers heard the roar of a low-flying jet. It was traveling at 440 miles per hour and went straight into the North Tower. It hit the building, instantly killing everyone on board—ninety-two passengers and crew, as well as five hijackers.

United Airlines Flight 175 left Logan Airport at 8:14 a.m. At 9:03 a.m., it hit floors seventy-eight through eighty-seven in the South Tower. It carried fifty-six passengers and crew and five hijackers.

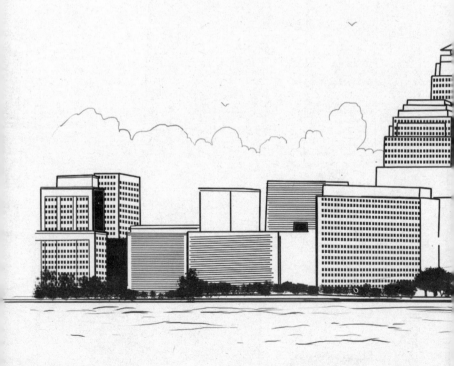

A third plane, American Airlines Flight 77, with sixty-four people (passengers plus crew) and five hijackers on board, took off from Washington's Dulles International Airport at 8:20 a.m. It slammed into the Pentagon building outside of Washington, DC, killing 125 workers, as well as everyone on the plane.

The fourth plane, United Airlines Flight 93, took off from Newark International Airport at 8:42 a.m. Soon after the terrorists seized control of the jet, passengers on Flight 93 heard on their cell phones about the other hijackings. They knew what was going to happen and decided to fight back. Some rushed the cockpit to

overpower the hijacker flying the plane. But he crashed it into a field in central Pennsylvania. The forty passengers and crew, as well as four hijackers, were killed. That plane had possibly been heading to Washington, DC, but because of the brave passengers, it never reached its target.

As news broke about the crash into the North Tower, many thought it was an accident. After the second plane hit the South Tower, it became clear that this was an attack. That's when *first responders*—rescue teams—began arriving. There were police, firefighters, and ambulance crews. They rushed into the buildings to save trapped workers and give first aid.

By this time, most office workers inside the towers had gotten out. (The best guess is that between eight and twelve thousand escaped.) However, almost everyone on floors above the points of impact was trapped. Fortunately, one stairway did remain open in the South Tower, and because of that, eighteen people who were above the eighty-seventh floor did escape.

As for people on lower floors, some who could have gotten out more easily didn't. They stayed at their desk, often after being told it was safer inside than out on the streets. This was terrible advice. Of course, no one realized that the Twin Towers would collapse . . . or how soon it would happen.

At 9:59 a.m., the South Tower fell, killing

everyone inside and sending a tremendous cloud of dust and debris into the air. Less than half an hour later, at 10:28 a.m., the North Tower collapsed. Two thousand six hundred and six innocent people died.

In all, 2,977 victims died on September 11, 2001. The nineteen hijackers also died.

Failure to Communicate

On 9/11, twenty-three NYC policemen and 343 firefighters died at the Twin Towers. The number might have been lower if rescue workers had been able to communicate better. The two departments had different kinds of radios that couldn't "talk" to each other. Also, fire department radios did not work well inside the Twin Towers. The South Tower fell first. However, firefighters in the North Tower didn't know about it because the department couldn't reach them.

New York City has a special office to help out in major emergencies. However, it was located in a building that was damaged when the South Tower collapsed. So the agency couldn't help out when it was needed most.

An illustrated view of New Amsterdam (present-day New York City) from the harbor in the 1660s

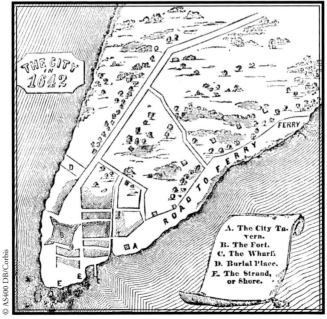

A map of New Amsterdam in 1642 showing early landmarks

Radio Row in New York City (seen above in 1936)
was demolished to make room for the towers.

Model of the World Trade Center
in 1964

The Empire State Building can b
seen from a partially completed fl
during construction (October 197

The towers rise as building continues in 1970.

The Twin Towers stand out against the New York City
skyline during a blackout on July 13, 1977.

High-wire artist Philippe Petit walks a tightrope
between the towers on August 7, 1974.

George Willig climbs the South Tower on May 26, 1977.

The shopping area under the World Trade Center (February 1979)

The trading floor of a stock brokerage firm, one of many businesses in the South Tower (February 1992)

Ambulances and fire trucks outside the World Trade Center after
an explosion in the parking garage on February 26, 1993

United Airlines Flight 175 crashes into the South Tower, minutes after the North Tower is hit on September 11, 2001.

The Pentagon, near Washington, DC, shortly after the September 11 attacks

President George W. Bush learns about the September 11
attacks from Chief of Staff Andrew Card.

A police scooter in the rubble after the September 11 attacks

A rescue dog at Ground Zero

Memorial in Union Square, New York City,
following the September 11 attacks

خاص بالجزيرة

بن لادن : ماتذوقه أمريكيا
لايقارن بعذاب العالم الاسلامي

Al Qaeda leader Osama bin Laden gives a televised
speech from a secret location (October 7, 2001)

Memorial lights commemorate the Twin Towers.
One World Trade Center can be seen on the left.

A memorial at the crash site of Flight 93 in Shanksville, Pennsylvania

The Survivor Tree, a pear tree tha survived the 9/11 attacks

One of the two reflecting pools where the towers once stood at the National September 11 Memorial

In the weeks after 9/11, firefighters, police, and construction workers continued searching for survivors. Sadly, they found no one. They also didn't fully realize how dangerous the polluted air was. In 2007, the names of people who became sick and died from working at Ground Zero began to be added to the official 9/11 death toll.

Missed Early Warnings

The attacks on 9/11 should not have been a complete surprise. The US government had warnings about a major terrorist plan.

In July 2001, the Federal Aviation Administration, the agency that watches out for trouble in the skies, told President George W. Bush that it had heard of "a significant threat" to passenger planes.

In August 2001, an Al Qaeda member was arrested at a flight school where he was learning to fly passenger jets.

That same month, an FBI agent in Arizona told his bosses that terrorists were in the United States taking flying lessons. No one followed up on his report.

The problem was no single government agency was in charge of going over all the information about terrorist plots. In fact, some agencies refused to share information with one another.

On August 6, 2001, President Bush received a report titled "Bin Laden Determined to Strike in US." The president thought the report was just saying that Al Qaeda was dangerous. That was something he already knew. Later, the president said that, had he been warned of Al Qaeda members in the United States, he would have reacted differently.

George W. Bush

CHAPTER 10
Why Did the Towers Fall?

In the days after the attack, one question people asked again and again was "How could those two huge buildings fall?"

There were many theories. The most common was that the intense heat of all the burning jet fuel melted the steel supports in the buildings' cores, as well as the curtain walls. That was not true.

Others said that the Trade Center had design faults.

That was not true, either.

Scientists and engineers studied the Twin Towers' design. These were strong, well-made buildings. The towers were not destroyed by the impact of either plane. Photographs taken right before the towers fell are proof of that. They show that the curtain wall was pushed in where the planes hit. However, the other sides of each building remained intact.

The jet fuel could not have burned hot enough to melt the steel. But fires inside the towers were hot enough to soften the steel in the core of each building. It became impossible for the softened steel to support the height of the floors above them. The inside core began to sag. The outside walls began to bend outward as the joints that linked the floors and walls gave way.

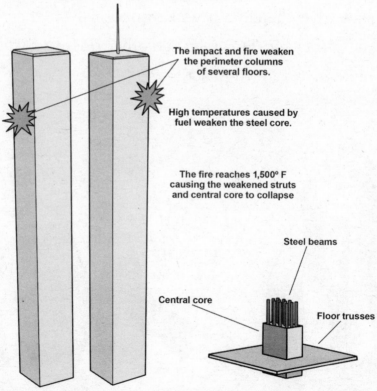

The impact and fire weaken the perimeter columns of several floors.

High temperatures caused by fuel weaken the steel core.

The fire reaches 1,500° F causing the weakened struts and central core to collapse

Steel beams

Central core

Floor trusses

Pilots in police helicopters could see the tops of the towers begin to tilt. They also reported that the top of the North Tower was glowing red-hot. Finally, the weight of the floors above the fires became too great. The upper floors "pancaked" or flattened onto one another. Floor after floor was crushed and turned to dust. It took about ten seconds for the South Tower to collapse. The North Tower went down in only about eight.

Clouds of blasted concrete and steel covered Lower Manhattan. The flaming wreckage of the buildings fell deep into the Twin Towers' subbasements. The fires burned for weeks. The smoke was even visible from outer space.

Another question often repeated was: "Could the terrorists have been stopped?"

Probably.

To prevent future attacks, there have been many changes in the way we live and travel since 9/11. At the end of 2001, the Department of Homeland Security was created to protect the United States from danger. It made many changes.

Before 9/11, security at airports was not tight. The hijackers had no trouble taking knives and box cutters onto four planes. They used those weapons to overpower flight crews. Since the attacks, travelers are thoroughly inspected at airports. Only ticket holders may go through the security checkpoint. Both travelers and their carry-on luggage are x-rayed for weapons or

liquids used to make bombs. Most travelers must remove their shoes, which are x-rayed for razor blades, explosives, and other weapons.

The cockpit doors on all airplanes are locked so no one can break in to where the pilots are.

Passenger ID is examined with names checked against a No Fly List. This list prevents some people who may be dangerous from boarding. The No Fly List has been criticized, because sometimes innocent travelers are delayed or even turned away.

In New York City, big office buildings began to require that workers show ID to enter and that visitors check in at security desks. Most government buildings in the United States now have metal detectors. Everyone must go through them before entering. The Department of Homeland Security also tries to make sure that terrorists do not come into the country at any of our border crossings.

Each year, Homeland Security gives out billions of dollars in grants to state and local governments to improve their ability to prevent terrorist attacks.

CHAPTER 11
The New World Trade Center

In the days following 9/11, New York City and the rest of the United States came together to grieve and show support for the country. In New York City, the stars and stripes were flown everywhere. Cars and motorcycles, bikes and boats, small towns and huge cities were flying the flag. People wore small flag pins. Flag decals were seen on construction workers' hard hats, car bumpers, trucks of every kind.

Right after the attack, the saddest sight in New York City was posters and fliers with pictures of missing persons. They were put up in the hope that somehow the people were still alive.

Memorials sprang up around New York City. Flowers, candles, balloons, cards, and letters to the victims of 9/11 were placed in public places and in nearby towns where the victims had lived. New York City firehouses put up pictures of the men from those stations who had died on 9/11.

The message was clear. The attack caused almost unbearable loss, but it could not defeat the spirit of Americans. The terrorists were not able to crush the country—or the city that had been so badly hurt. Now, instead of posters that said, "I♥NY," there were ones saying, "I♥NY More Than Ever."

Almost at once there was talk of a new World Trade Center to be built, with a memorial honoring all the victims. But how should it be handled? Should the Twin Towers be rebuilt exactly as they were? Some thought so. Others, often those who had lost loved ones on September 11, said that the area where the towers fell was sacred ground. It was the final resting place of more than 1,100 victims whose remains were never found. Nothing should be built there.

In the end, the decision was to set aside land for a museum and memorial. The rest of the area would become new office towers.

In July 2002, there was a worldwide contest to design a master plan for the entire sixteen-acre site. From over four hundred entries, a panel of architects and city planners picked seven finalists. In February 2003, architect Daniel Libeskind was chosen to carry out his plan. He called it "Memory Foundations." It featured a tower, with

Daniel Libeskind

a spire, that was 1,776 feet tall that became known as Freedom Tower. It would be the tallest building in the United States. Its height referred to the year 1776, when the American colonies declared their independence from England and became a free country. Today, the finished building is called One World Trade Center.

In April 2003, another contest was announced. This was for the design of the memorial and the 9/11 museum. The memorial area was to take up eight acres, including the ones where the Twin Towers had once stood. Anyone over the age of eighteen could enter the contest. Five thousand two hundred and one proposals came in. Judging all the entries took nine months.

The winner was "Reflecting Absence" by architect Michael Arad. One of the judges was a famous architect named Maya Lin. She said Arad "made something positive out of the void." (*Void* is another word for a deep hole.)

The names of all the victims were inscribed on the rims of two giant fountains. Names were grouped in a meaningful way. Family members appear together. So do friends and coworkers.

The waist-high walls of the fountains outline the footprints of the Twin Towers. Water cascades down all four sides of each and collects in a reflecting pool at the bottom. As it grows dark, the names are lit so that even on the blackest night, they all can be seen.

Arad's original proposal for the plaza was too bare. The judges urged him to work with a landscape architect. They decided to surround the memorial waterfalls with a grove of more than four hundred oak trees. This made the plaza greener and more welcoming.

The Survivor Tree

Within the grove of oaks, one tree stands out. It is a pear tree and a true survivor of 9/11. The tree was one of many in the outdoor plaza of the Twin Towers. All the others were burned or crushed when the buildings fell. Hardly more than a stump was left of one remaining pear tree. But it was still alive. The tree was sent to a nursery in the Bronx, New York, where it grew new branches. In December 2010, the pear tree, now called the Survivor Tree, was placed among the oaks. It is thirty feet high. Each spring, it is the first tree to bloom. Its beautiful white flowers are a sign of life at a place where there was so much death and destruction.

Because the two fountains are at ground level, some of the space for museum exhibits was placed under the footprints of the two towers.

The finished memorial area is quiet and restful. Large crowds of visitors walk through the lines of oak trees to the fountains. People speak softly. The waterfalls splash quietly. The wind rustles the leaves of the trees. It is truly a place of remembering.

CHAPTER 12
The Museum

Figuring out the design of the 9/11 Memorial Museum was also complicated. Because the two fountains are so big, much of the exhibit space in the museum is seventy feet underground.

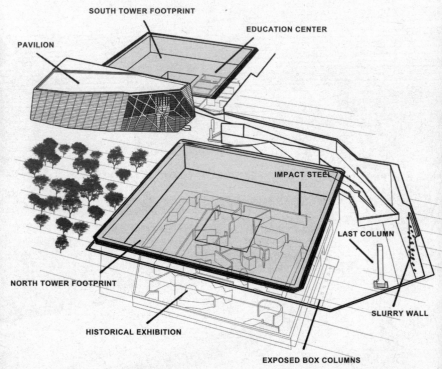

SOUTH TOWER FOOTPRINT

EDUCATION CENTER

PAVILION

IMPACT STEEL

LAST COLUMN

NORTH TOWER FOOTPRINT

SLURRY WALL

HISTORICAL EXHIBITION

EXPOSED BOX COLUMNS

Going to most museums is fun. It is a chance to see beautiful art or learn about science. The 9/11 Memorial Museum is different. It focuses on a terrible day in history, and much of what is shown is difficult to look at and learn about.

When visitors arrive at the museum, they go down one level and walk through a darkened hall that echoes with taped voices of people saying where they were and what they heard or saw on the morning of September 11, 2001.

The witnesses' words are also lit up on nearby panels. At the bottom of the ramp, visitors can look down onto the main exhibit floor. A section of the massive slurry wall, which still holds back the waters of the Hudson River, is nearby.

Then visitors take an escalator farther down. Next to the escalator are the Survivors' Stairs. On 9/11, countless people went down them to safety. Many remembered a policeman telling them, "Run down these stairs and then run for your lives."

Many objects in the museum are massive and weigh thousands of pounds. There is a giant motor that powered one of the elevators, a battered EMS truck, giant, twisted I-beams, and huge pieces of structural steel.

A fire truck that belonged to Ladder 3 Company is also there. It had its cab sheared off by falling pieces of the towers. What remains is battered. Part of the ladder is stretched and twisted.

Eleven members from this firehouse in New York City's East Village went to the Twin Towers on 9/11, and all of them died there.

Years earlier, these important objects had been moved from Ground Zero. They were kept in a hangar at John F. Kennedy International Airport. In 2008, the largest and heaviest things were brought back to where the Twin Towers had stood. Each piece was carefully lowered by crane into its place in the future museum. Then the roof of the museum was closed and covered by the memorial plaza.

In front of the slurry wall is the Last Column. It weighs fifty-eight tons and was the last piece of the Twin Towers to be taken from Ground Zero. It is covered with messages workers wrote on it during the cleanup efforts.

There are also many small items on display: eyeglasses, house keys, company ID cards, wallets, and shoes. There are firefighters' helmets.

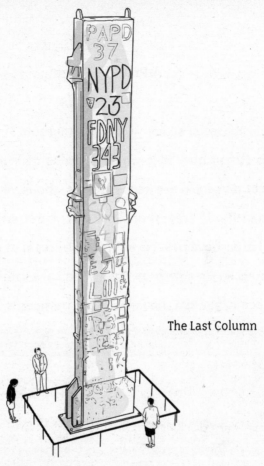

The Last Column

Some look like they could still be used, but one is broken and split apart.

In all, the museum has ten thousand objects, large and small, that tell the story of the attacks on the Twin Towers and on Washington, DC.

A Private Place

A special space within the museum is not open to the public. It is where remains of some of the victims of 9/11 are kept—victims who have not been identified. One thousand one hundred thirteen victims have never been found. A team of scientists from NYC's Office of Chief Medical Examiner tests each of the ten thousand bone fragments for a DNA

match. Their hope is to identify more victims. They rarely get a match, however.

The scientists' workplace is connected to a private area known as the Reflection Room. It is for 9/11 families. There, they can be near the place where their loved ones were last alive. On the wall outside this area is a quotation from Virgil: "No day shall erase you from the memory of time."

FROM THE MEMORY OF TIME

Virgil

One World Trade Center

These are all bits and pieces of the larger story of September 11, 2001. A visit to the museum offers a glimpse into the lives of the ordinary people who worked at the Twin Towers and

Pentagon, the first responders, and the passengers and crews on the doomed planes.

It reminds all of us to think of the day and the victims, so that their memory will never be erased.

Timeline of the Twin Towers

1960	David Rockefeller encourages Port Authority to build skyscrapers in lower Manhattan
1961	Early plan is devised for a World Trade Center
1966	Plan is approved for two giant skyscrapers called the North and South Towers
	Old buildings on the site are torn down
1969	By spring, part of the steel skeleton of the North Tower is in place
1970	In December, first tenants move into the North Tower
1971	In September, tenants begin moving into the South Tower
1973	Official opening day of the Twin Towers is on April 4
1974	In August, Philippe Petit walks across a tightrope between the towers
1977	In May, George Willig climbs up the outside of the South Tower
1993	In February, a van with explosives damages the underground levels of the North Tower and kills six people
1997	In November, Ramzi Yousef is convicted for the attack (he is currently serving a life sentence in prison)
2001	On September 11, terrorists hijack four commercial planes, with three hitting their intended targets: the North and South Towers in New York City and the Pentagon building outside Washington, DC
2002	In July, a worldwide contest is held for the design of a new World Trade Center at the same site
2003	Daniel Libeskind is chosen to carry out his plan for the redesign
	Another contest is held to design the memorial to the victims and the 9/11 Memorial Museum, with Michael Arad as the winner
2011	The memorial is unveiled
2014	The new One World Trade Center is officially opened
	The 9/11 Memorial Museum opens

Timeline of the World

1930	The Chrysler Building in New York City opens
1931	The Empire State Building in New York City opens
1963	Civil rights march on Washington, DC, where Dr. Martin Luther King Jr. gives his "I Have a Dream" speech
	President John F. Kennedy is assassinated
1964	Beatlemania hits the United States
1967	Nearly one hundred thousand people gather in Washington, DC, to protest the Vietnam War
1969	Astronaut Neil Armstrong walks on the moon
	In August, the three-day rock music festival known as Woodstock is held in upstate New York
1974	US president Richard Nixon resigns
	The Sears Tower in Chicago, which is taller than either of the Twin Towers, is finished
1975	Microsoft is founded by Bill Gates and Paul Allen
1976	The United States celebrates its two hundredth birthday
1977	*Star Wars* opens in movie theaters
1989	The Berlin Wall is torn down
1991	The Soviet Union collapses
1994	The Channel Tunnel ("Chunnel") opens, connecting England and France
2002	Kelly Clarkson wins the first *American Idol*
2009	In January, Barack Obama becomes the first African American US president
2010	Burj Khalifa building in Dubai becomes the tallest building in the world

Bibliography

*Books for young readers

Blais, Allison, and Lynn Rasic. *A Place of Remembrance: Official Book of the National September 11 Memorial.* Washington, DC: National Geographic, 2011.

* Frank, Mitch. *Understanding September 11th: Answering Questions About the Attacks on America.* New York: Viking, 2002.

Gillespie, Angus Kress. *Twin Towers: The Life of New York City's World Trade Center.* New Brunswick, NJ: Rutgers UP, 1999.

Jacobson, Sid, and Ernie Colón. *The 9/11 Report: A Graphic Adaptation.* New York: Hill and Wang, 2006.

* Langley, Andrew. *September 11: Attack on America.* Minneapolis: Compass Point Books, 2006.

Robins, Anthony. *The World Trade Center.* Englewood, FL: Pineapple Press, 1987.